ANIMALS

A TEMPLAR BOOK

Devised and produced by The Templar Company plc
Pippbrook Mill, London Road, Dorking, Surrey RH4 1JE

Copyright © 1992 by The Templar Company plc
Illustrations copyright © 1992 by The Templar Company plc

This edition produced for Bookmart Ltd

Designed by Jane Louise Hunt
Printed and bound in Malaysia

ISBN 1 870956 80 X

FIND THE DIFFERENCE

ANIMALS

Written by Andrew Charman
Illustrated by Sallie Reason

CONTENTS

TEMPLAR

4

There are 2,800 different kinds of birds in the world.
They live everywhere, from the frozen Antarctic to the steamy
jungles of South America. Here are just a few of them.

The picture above contains 10 things that make it different from the picture on the left. A bird may have caught its dinner or changed position. Can you find all 10? The answers are on page 20.

Insects come in all shapes, sizes and colours. There are many different kinds and they can be found almost everywhere. Here, you can see moths, butterflies, bugs, beetles, weevils and many more.

The picture above contains 15 things that make it different from the one on the left. Can you see what they are? Turn to the answers on page 20 to check if you've found them all.

8

In the Arctic of the North and the Antarctic of the South it is almost always freezing, and it is dark for much of the year. Here are some of the birds and animals that live in these harsh places.

The picture above contains 12 things that make it different from the picture on the left. Are you sharp-eyed enough to find them? Turn to page 20 to see if you have found them all.

10

The Australian forests cover only a small area in that vast country,
but they are teeming with life. Many of the creatures that live there are
not found anywhere else in the world.

In the picture above, there are 14 hidden creatures. Many of them have markings and colours which help them to blend in with the leaves and flowers of their forest home. Can you find them?

The coral reefs of the tropical seas are busy and exciting places.
The fish and other creatures that live in them are the most colourful in
the world. Although they look like plants, corals are animals.

There are 15 creatures hidden among the coral in this scene.
Can you see where they are? On page 21 you will be able to learn
their names and find out where they are hiding.

There are over 4,000 different kinds of mammals in the world.
They live almost everywhere. Mice, monkeys, whales, kangaroos,
rats and human beings are all types of mammals.

Here are just a few of the world's mammals. There are 12 differences between the picture above and the one on the left. Can you find them? Turn to page 22 to see if you've found all of them.

Deserts are not pleasant places in which to live. It hardly ever rains, the sun scorches the land during the daytime, and it is bitterly cold at night. Here are some of the animals that live in the world's deserts.

The desert scene shown above contains 15 things that make it different from the picture on the left. Can you find them? Turn to the answers on page 22 to see if you have found them all.

There are many record breaking creatures on earth. Pictured here are just a few of them. They include the tallest animal, the biggest bird, the fastest creature on earth, and the most poisonous.

This is the last of our find the difference quizzes. How well have you done? Test your skills by finding the 11 things in the picture above that make it different from the one on the left.

THE DIFFERENCES

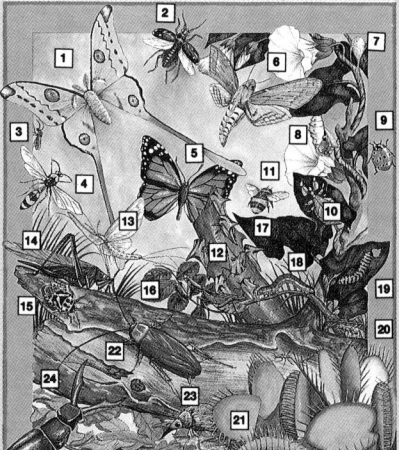

Beautiful Birds

1. Toucan – no change.
2. Lovebird – no change.
3 The motmot has gained another long tail feather.
4. The flamingo is now standing on both legs.
5. Gouldian finch – no change.
6. The swan has changed from a Bewick's swan to a mute swan, a different species.
7. The hoopoe's crest has folded.
8. Peafowl – no change.
9. The hummingbird is feeding on nectar, and a new flower has appeared.
10. Wren – no change.
11. The female hornbill is in the nest hole. She has stuck out her bill to take food from the male hornbill.
12. The snowy owl has closed an eye.
13. Purple heron – no change.
14. The pelican now has some fish in its huge bill.
15. The emperor penguin's chick has moved his head.
16. The puffin has lost his summer plumage. The colours helped him to attract a mate.

Incredible Insects

1. Silk moth – no change.
2. Tiger beetle – no change.
3. Gnat – no change.
4. Vespid wasp – no change.
5. The viceroy butterfly has turned into a monarch butterfly.
6. Hawk moth – no change.
7. Frog hoppers usually hide in this frothy substance.
8. A butterfly is emerging from the chrysalis.
9. The seven-spot ladybird has become an eyed ladybird.
10. The leaf insect has moved.
11. Bumble bee – no change.
12. There is another thorn bug.
13. Mayfly – no change.
14. Bush cricket – no change.
15. The green shield bug has become a different kind of bug.
16. The mantis has caught a fly.
17. There is another thorn.
18. The caterpillar has moved.
19. The cinnabar caterpillar has eaten away part of its leaf.
20. The ant has found a leaf.
21. The flytrap has caught a fly.
22. The cockroach has moved one of its long antennae.
23. Weevil – no change.
24. One stag beetle has gone.

Land of Ice

1. Ivory gull – no change.
2. This ptarmigan has grown brown feathers.
3. Snowy owl – no change.
4. The caribou has longer antlers.
5. Musk ox – no change.
6. The wolf has turned from white to grey.
7. An Arctic hare has appeared.
8. One of the emperor penguins now has an egg to look after.
9. One of the emperor penguins has gone. Perhaps it has gone fishing!
10. The markings and colour of the banded seal have changed.
11. The ice has broken and another seal has appeared.
12. Arctic fox – no change.
13. A polar bear cub has appeared. It will stay with its mother for a year.
14. The walrus's tusks have grown a little longer.
15. Sheath bill – no change.
16. Another lemming has joined the group.
17. The macaroni penguin has grown more head feathers.

THE HIDDEN ANIMALS

In the Forest

1. The boobook owl is named after its call.
2. Rainbow lorikeets live in large and noisy flocks of up to 100 birds. They nest in holes, high above the ground.
3. Red wallabies eat leaves.
4. The striped possum lives in trees and comes out at night.
5. Tasmanian devils come out at night to hunt small animals.
6. The spiny anteater scuttles along the forest floor. It picks up insects on its sticky tongue.
7. Kookaburras are famous for their noisy, laughlike call.
8. Koalas spend most of their time in the trees eating leaves. They eat over 1 kg of leaves every day.
9. Carpet pythons hunt at night. They are not venomous, but kill small animals with their sharp teeth.
10. The tiny Queensland blossom bat flys from flower to flower feeding on nectar.
11. Wombats live in burrows that stretch more than 12 metres from the entrance.
12. The frilled lizard's collar usually lies folded against its neck. When the lizard is alarmed, the collar becomes erect giving the animal a startling appearance.
13. Crimson chats eat insects.
14. The male lyrebird uses his long tail to attract a mate.

Down among the Coral

1. These bright fish are Moorish idols.
2. Those waving arms belong to the blue-ringed octopus. It is one of the world's most dangerous animals.
3. The seahorse clings to the coral with its curly tail. It usually lives in shallow waters.
4. The rainbow parrotfish comes from the western Atlantic Ocean, and can be 1 metre in length.
5. The kihikihi comes from the Indian and Pacific Oceans.
6. The moray eel lurks in crevices and grabs squid and cuttlefish as they pass by.
7. The redfish sits on the sea bed during the day.
8. The red sea anemone looks like a plant, but it is an animal with a mouth and tentacles.
9. The crown of thorns starfish eats the corals.
10. This beautiful fish is a mandarinfish. It lives on the sea bed among the coral.
11. The clownfish lives among the tentacles of the anemone.
12. This is a giant clam. It can measure almost 1 metre long.
13. Weedy seadragons are camouflaged to look like bits of seaweed.
14. The clown triggerfish hides in crevices when frightened.
15. The nautilus.

MORE DIFFERENCES

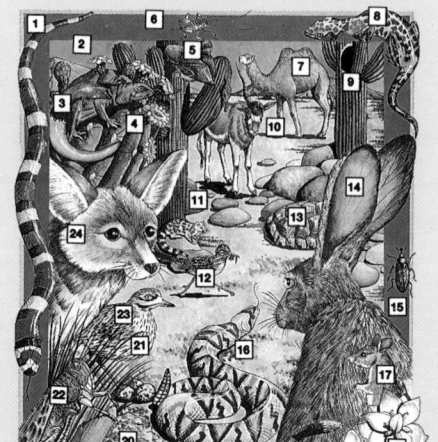

Magnificent Mammals

1. The night monkey has curled its long tail around the branch.
2. The red giant squirrel has leapt from the tree.
3. Tree pangolin – no change.
4. Giraffe – no change.
5. The zebra's stripes have changed.
6. The giant panda has found some bamboo to eat.
7. The ermine has grown a brown coat for the summer.
8. Spring hare – no change.
9. The star-nosed mole came up to see where he was. Now he's gone.
10. The hamster has stored most of its meal in its cheek pouches.
11. The lemur has a young one riding on its back.
12. Wolf – no change.
13. The deer has grown antlers.
14. The leopard has turned into a snow leopard.
15. The lesser horseshoe bat on the left has become a common long-eared bat.
16. The grey squirrel has turned into a red squirrel.
17. Shrew – no change.

Creatures of the Desert

1. The coral snake has become a kingsnake.
2. The sparrowhawk has left.
3. The chuckwalla lizard is now catching a fly.
4. There is another flower.
5. Leaf-nosed bat – no change.
6. Dune cricket – no change.
7. Dromedary camels have one hump. This one has changed to a two-humped camel.
8. Night lizard – no change.
9. The elf owls have gone.
10. The addax has lost an antler.
11. Genet – no change.
12. The roadrunner has caught a lizard.
13. The tortoise is hiding.
14. Jack rabbit – no change.
15. Weevil – no change.
16. The rattlesnake has eaten the small rodent.
17. Gerbil – no change.
18. The yucca moth has left.
19. The jerboa's tail is shorter.
20. The toad has gone.
21. Another egg has appeared.
22. The locust has been eating.
23. Cactus wren – no change.
24. Fennec fox – no change.

Record Breakers

1. A pygmy marmoset (smallest primate) has appeared.
2. Goliath beetle – no change.
3. Sloth – no change.
4. Another Arctic tern (longest flier) has appeared.
5. The giraffe has more spots. It is the tallest animal.
6. Emperor moth – no change.
7. The cheetah's leg has moved. It is the fastest animal.
8. The elephant (largest land mammal) has two long tusks.
9. This man has aged.
10. The ostrich's egg is hatching. It is the largest bird.
11. The bumblebee bat (smallest mammal) has disappeared.
12. Capybara – no change.
13. Mouse – no change.
14. There are two poison-dart frogs (most poisonous animals).
15. Shrew – no change.
16. The king cobra (longest poisonous snake) has stuck out its tongue.
17. Hercules beetle – no change.
18. The bee hummingbird (smallest bird) has changed from a female to a male.